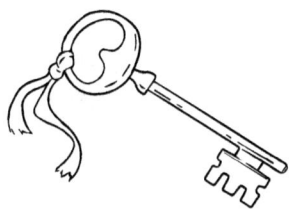

WORLDVIEW GUIDE

JANE EYRE

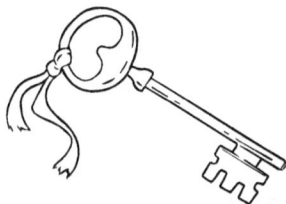

Amanda Ryan

canonpress
Moscow, Idaho

Published by Canon Press
P.O. Box 8729, Moscow, Idaho 83843
800.488.2034 | www.canonpress.com

Amanda Ryan, *Worldview Guide for Jane Eyre*
Copyright © 2017 by Amanda Ryan.
For the Canon Classics edition of the novel (2017), visit www.canonpress.com/
books/canon-classics.

Cover design by James Engerbretson
Cover illustration by Forrest Dickison
Interior design by Valerie Anne Bost and James Engerbretson

Printed in the United States of America.

All Scripture quotations taken from the Authorized Version.

A free end-of-book test and answer key are available for download at
www.canonpress.com/ClassicsQuizzes

Ryan, Amanda, author.
Jane Eyre worldview guide / Amanda Ryan.
Moscow, Idaho : Canon Press, [2017] | Includes bibliographical
    references and index.
LCCN 2019011334 | ISBN 1591282489 (paperback : alk. paper)
LCSH: Brontè, Charlotte, 1816-1855. Jane Eyre.
LCC PR4167.J5 R93 2017 | DDC 823/.8--dc23
LC record available at https://lccn.loc.gov/2019011334

17 18 19 20 21 22   9 8 7 6 5 4 3 2 1

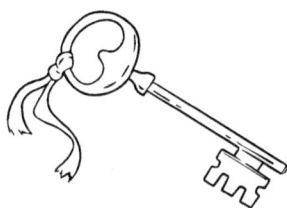

CONTENTS

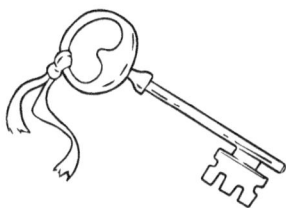

INTRODUCTION

In a letter to her literary advisor, Charlotte Brontë once described her new creation of *Jane Eyre* as a "mere domestic novel," one which "discusses no subject of public interest" and would most likely "seem trivial to men of large views and solid attainments."[1] In Victorian England, the domestic domain was too small and insignificant a world to catch the interest of the public and people of importance.

It is true that *Jane Eyre* is not overtly concerned with the public interests of her day. The novel focuses on the life of the mind and heart of a woman on the fringe of society. By doing this, Brontë introduced the literary world to a sphere it had yet to see and, ironically, one larger than it

---

1. All quotations from Charlotte Brontë and Richard J. Dunn, *Jane Eyre: An Authoritative Text, Backgrounds, Criticism* (New York: Norton, 1971), 419.

could contain.[2] In Jane's struggle, the novel presents an argument, persuasive mainly through its pathos, against the 19th century norms of classism, gender roles, marriage, passion versus restraint, and convention versus truth.

2. Lyndall Gordon, *Charlotte Brontë, a Passionate Life* (New York: W.W. Norton, 1995), 163.

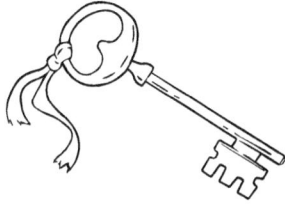

THE WORLD AROUND

Jane Eyre was published in 1847 during the early stages of the Victorian Era. During this time, the Industrial Revolution had reached its peak and England was eating its fruits (and learning how to deal with its less savory consequences). With the increase of factories, job numbers increased, cities like London blossomed, and the middle class expanded. Technological improvements allowed the printing industry to explode with productivity. Books became cheaper to produce and more readily available to all levels of the public. Literacy rates improved and the demand for literature, and novels in particular, increased. So did the supply. The 19th century saw an unprecedented number of novelists, and England introduced some of its most beloved. Charles Dickens was at the height of his literary career when *Jane Eyre* was published.[3] Other

---

3. Christine L. Krueger, *Encyclopedia of British Writers, 19th and 20th Centuries* (New York: Facts On File, 2003), 88.

novelists of the time included Sir Walter Scott, William Makepeace Thackeray, Elizabeth Gaskell, and Anthony Trollope. The notorious philanderer Lord Byron had left his mark on the literary world with the introduction of the Byronic Hero, the sympathetic villain or the anti-hero, and his romantic ideal of the artist as misunderstood.

Slavery had been abolished from the British Empire for nearly a decade but the conversation about human rights and social justice continued, spanning into other issues, such as a woman's place in society. Across the seas in America, the Women's Rights movements amassed their forces, and Elizabeth Cady Stanton would begin lobbying for the vote.

The moral climate of Victorian England is marked by rigid ideals and a suffocating view of femininity. Women could not enter higher education, and vocations beyond mother, teacher, or governess were not available to them. Depictions of women in the English Novel up to that point were, for the most part, images of helpless beauties whose virtues were more intuitive than principled (such as Samuel Richardson's *Pamela; Or a Virtue Rewarded*). When *Jane Eyre* came on scene, the novel put a finger on the pulse of Victorian women, who, like Jane, quietly longed for more than "making puddings and knitting stockings."

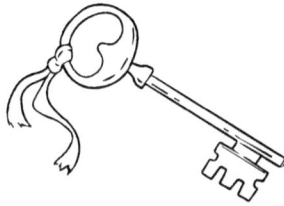

ABOUT THE AUTHOR

Charlotte Brontë was born in 1816, and her life provides some interesting parallels to *Jane Eyre*. She grew up in Haworth, England, a small village once known for its wool production surrounded by moors. Charlotte's early life was fraught with tragedy. When she was five years old her mother died of cancer, leaving Charlotte, her four sisters and a brother to be raised by their severe father, Patrick Brontë, a clergyman with ascetic beliefs. When Charlotte was eight years old, she and her sisters were sent to the Clergy Daughter's School at Cowan Bridge. Under the harsh, unhygienic conditions of the school, the health of Charlotte's sisters Maria and Elizabeth dwindled, and they both eventually died of tuberculosis.

After these untimely deaths, Charlotte and her brother and sisters were schooled at home. Here they indulged their imaginations by adventuring in the moors, reading widely, putting on plays, and writing about imaginary worlds. What began as stories about Charles and Arthur Wellesley, the Duke of Wellington's sons, quickly developed into an ongoing saga featuring the "Duke Zamorna"—a philanderer of Byronic proportions who lives in the dark realm of "Angria."[4]

When Charlotte was nineteen years old, she began teaching at Roe Head School. All the while she cherished dreams of writing and jotted down poetry as well as stories of her beloved Zamorna.

Years later, in 1842, Charlotte and her sister Emily attended Pensionnat Heger, a school in Brussels. There Charlotte formed an obsessive infatuation with her Rhetoric teacher. When communication was cut off, Charlotte went back to England and began writing in earnest. She and her sisters published a book of poems under male pseudonyms in the hopes of gaining more success and staving off accusations of being unfeminine. Around that time, Charlotte wrote her first novel, *The Professor.* This book was rejected several times and would not be published until after her death. Brontë eventually wrote *Jane Eyre*, which was published under a pseudonym, and was immediately received with acclaim, as well as suspicion. Eyebrows were raised as to the gender of the author, "Currer Bell." One critic claimed that if the work was written by a man, it was wonderful, but if written by

4. Carol A. Bock, "Charlotte Brontë," Poetry Foundation, accessed December 8, 2016, https://www.poetryfoundation.org/poems-and-poets/poets/detail/charlotte-bronte.

a woman, "odious."[5] The questions of femininity and the role of women in society followed the book wherever it went, and they followed the author too. Charlotte would continue to address these subjects even more pointedly in her subsequent novels *Shirley* and *Villette*.

She married Arthur Bell in 1854. In letter to a friend, Charlotte comments on her status as a married lady, "It is a solemn and strange and perilous thing for a woman to become a wife."[6] She died the next year at the early age of thirty-eight, possibly due to complications with her pregnancy.

---

5. Krueger, 40.
6. Ibid, 39.

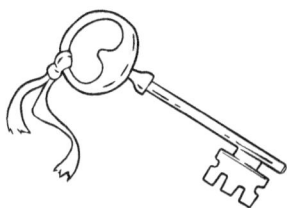

WHAT OTHER NOTABLES SAID

Since its publication, *Jane Eyre* has received mixed reviews. George Henry Lewes, one of the novel's first reviewers, expressed some hang-ups with the "machinery" of the novel, but praised it for its realism. "Reality," he writes, "deep significant reality—is the great characteristic of the book.... It is soul speaking to soul; it is an utterance from the depths of a struggling, suffering, much-enduring spirit: *suspiria de profundis!*"[7]

The ever good-humored C.S. Lewis, who praised the book as "magnificent,"[8] was a little more skeptical about the realism of Brontë's male characters and her ideas of happily ever after. In a letter to his brother, Lewis writes:

---

7. "Review of Jane Eyre," *Fraser's Magazine for Town and Country* 36 (December 1847): 690-694.

8. C. S. Lewis, *Collected Letters of C.S. Lewis, Vol. I: Family Letters 1905–1931,* ed. Walter Hooper (San Francisco: HarperCollins, 2004), 77.

> Part of the interest lies in seeing in the most (ap-
> parently) preposterous male characters how quite
> ordinary people look through the eyes of a shy,
> naive, inflexibly upright, intelligent little woman of
> the mouse-like governessy type. It opens vistas—
> how you or I look to Maureen's friend "Fuller"
> or how we may all have looked to "Smudge"....
> Particularly delicious is her idea of conjugal bliss
> when she says almost on the last page, "We talk, I
> believe, all day."[9]

On a more serious note, Virginia Woolf suggests that it is the poetry of Jane's voice that makes the novel so compelling.[10] "As we open Jane Eyre once more we cannot stifle the suspicion that we shall find her world of imagination as antiquated, mid-Victorian, and out of date as the parsonage on the moor, a place only to be visited by the curious, only preserved by the pious. So we open *Jane Eyre*; and in two pages every doubt is swept clean from our minds."[11]

9. C.S. Lewis, *The Collected Letters of C.S. Lewis, Vol. 2: Books, Broadcasts, and the War 1931-1949*, ed. Walter Hooper (New York: HarperCollins Publishers, 2007), 291.

10. Carol A. Bock, "Charlotte Brontë."

11. Katerina Koutsantoni, *Virginia Woolf's Common Reader* (Farnham, England: Ashgate, 2009), 106.

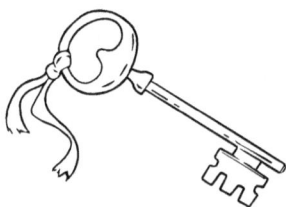

SETTING, CHARACTERS, AND PLOT SUMMARY

- *Setting: Early 19th century England.*
- *Jane Eyre:* Protagonist.
- *Mr. Reed:* Jane's deceased Uncle. On his death-bed, he asked his wife to take care of Jane as one of her own children.
- *Mrs. Reed:* Jane's cruel Aunt who neglects her husband's wishes to take care of Jane.
- *John Reed:* Jane's cousin who has a sadistic love of bullying. He eventually commits suicide after draining much of his family's funds.
- *Eliza Reed:* Jane's pietistic cousin who eventually becomes a nun.
- *Georgiana Reed:* Jane's gushy, overly emotional cousin.

- *Bessie Lee:* The children's nurse and maid at Gateshead. She is a kind of friend to Jane and eventually marries Robert Leaven.
- *Robert Leaven:* The coachman who informs Jane of John Reed's death. He takes Jane to see her Aunt Reed on her deathbed.
- *Mr. Brocklehurst:* The greasy pietist and clergyman, also owner and founder of the Lowood school.
- *Maria Temple:* A kind teacher and role model to Jane at Lowood.
- *Miss Scatcherd:* Another teacher at Lowood. A sour presence.
- *Helen Burns:* Jane's first true friend at Lowood. Helen is a saintly figure and influential to Jane's ideas of perseverance and Christian duty.
- *Mrs. Fairfax:* The housekeeper of Thornfield. A kind spinster-companion to Jane.
- *Adele:* The Parisian illegitimate child of Rochester's former lover, Celine Varens.
- *Edward Rochester:* A bombastic, manipulative ladies' man and Jane's main love interest.
- *Grace Poole:* The mysterious servant at Thornfield frequently blamed for the strange laughter Jane hears and little accidents that occur there.
- *Blanche Ingram:* The beautiful woman courted by Rochester to make Jane jealous.

- *Bertha Mason Rochester:* The crazy woman locked up in Rochester's attic. She is Rochester's first wife from Jamaica and is responsible for the fires and other accidents that occur at Thornfield.
- *Richard Mason:* Bertha Mason's brother, Rochester's brother-in-law.
- *St. John Rivers (pronounced "Sinjun"):* The young and stoic clergyman who turns out to be Jane's cousin.
- *Diana Rivers:* St. John's sister, Jane's cousin.
- *Mary Rivers:* St. John's sister, Jane's cousin.
- *Hannah:* The Rivers' maid.
- *Rosamund Oliver:* The beautiful but fluffy-headed woman with whom St. John is in love.

The story opens with sensitive, ten-year-old Jane being bullied by her fourteen-year-old cousin, John Reed. When he smacks her head with a book, Jane retaliates and pummels him with all her might. This incident proves to Aunt Reed her suspicions about Jane—Jane's character is passionate and unrestrained and it must be reformed. Shortly after, Aunt Reed sends Jane to the harsh and unsanitary Lowood Institution with the aim of getting rid of her. In this severe environment, Jane learns how to rule her spirit and how to deal with the abuses caused by the people around her.

Jane excels in her studies and eventually takes a position as governess at Thornfield Hall, a gloomy castle surrounded by moors and filled with ominous vibes and mysterious sounds. At Thornfield, Jane meets the broody, fat-foreheaded Edward Rochester, who takes her into his cryptic confidence. Sparks fly. They nurse secret infatuations for each other. Rochester creatively attempts to bring the situation to a crisis by courting the buxom brunette, Blanche Ingram, and then disguising himself as a fortune-teller in the hopes Jane will confess her true feelings for him. What's a girl to do?

When Jane confronts Rochester, he professes his love and they get engaged. However, their happiness is short-lived, for their wedding ceremony is interrupted with an important announcement made by Rochester's *brother-in-law*—Rochester has a wife! She's living in the attic!

Although Rochester pleads with Jane to stay with him, her conscience and her sense of self-respect forbid her. She runs away. Penniless, starving, and near the point of death, Jane is taken in by St. John Rivers, a clergyman, and his sisters. With their help, Jane gets back on her feet. In a twist of fate, Jane discovers she is related to the Rivers, and that she has in fact gained a large inheritance of money. In the meantime, St. John, noticing Jane's hard work ethic and durable spirit, proposes to her. "You were formed for labour not for love," (354) he says—stoic-speak for missionary material. Still in love with Rochester, and not exactly swept off her feet, Jane refuses.

Providence prompts her to go back to Rochester. When she does, she discovers that Thornfield has been burned down, Bertha killed in the fire, and that Rochester is crippled and his wealth diminished. The road has been paved for them to live happily ever after together, which they proceed to do.

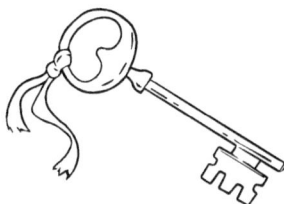

WORLDVIEW ANALYSIS

Probably the most popular issue surrounding *Jane Eyre* is the "feminist question." Does the novel skew gender roles and contradict a biblical understanding of femininity, or is something else going on? This question has hounded the book since its publication, and, unsurprisingly, *Jane Eyre* has been commandeered by many a feminist scholar. However, feminists have also claimed the works of Jane Austen, Anne Bradstreet, Shakespeare, and the Good Lord Himself for their agenda. Just because the feminists plant their flag on an author does not make that author a feminist. For a Christian reader, it is instead more helpful to ask whether or not the virtues being normalized and applauded in *Jane Eyre* are actually biblical virtues. Are her ideas about of romance, marriage, and gender roles faithful to a biblical vision? Or are they foolish?

A key to approaching these questions is to consider the novel's form. In the world of literary criticism, *Jane Eyre* is considered a *bildungsroman*, a fancy German word which basically means a "coming of age" tale. In this kind of story the protagonist overcomes spiritual hardship and grows up despite the hard soil of a restrictive society. The story is about who or what the main character becomes at the end, and this determines the novel's outlook.

It is also important to note what Charlotte wanted to accomplish by creating the character Jane Eyre. She wanted to introduce a new kind of heroine. According to Elizabeth Gaskell, Brontë's friend and biographer,

> [Charlotte] once told her sisters that they were wrong—even morally wrong—in making their heroine beautiful as a matter of course. They replied that it was impossible to make a heroine interesting on any other terms. Her answer was, "I will prove to you that you are wrong; I will show you a heroine as plain and as small as myself, who shall be as interesting as any of yours."[12]

And she did. Instead of using the what was then stereotypical heroine, the beauty, the one who needs a Prince to come after her, who does the right thing not knowing exactly why, Brontë creates a heroine who lacks physical beauty, but whose actions are principled; one who doesn't need a prince but gets one anyways.[13]

---

12. Elizabeth Gaskell and Elisabeth Jay, *The Life of Charlotte Brontë* (London: Penguin Books, 1997), 215-216.
13. It's since become the main staple of heroine—although in some movies they'll still get a pretty actor but give her glasses and *say* she's

The bildungsroman allowed Charlotte Brontë the space to show the development of a flawed, plain girl into a strong, mature woman whose mind and spirit are what make her beautiful. At the start of the story, we see that Jane has a sharp eye for the injustice (12) around her and a desire to be an agent of its correction. She declares, "When we are struck at without a reason, we should strike back again very hard; I am sure we should—so hard as to teach the person who struck us never to do it again" (50) To make matters worse, Jane is unable to fit in with the people around her (12) but deeply longs to be loved and approved of. In a conversation with Helen Burns, Jane confesses, "Look here; to gain some real affection from you, or Miss Temple, or any other whom I truly love, I would willingly submit to have the bone of my arm broken, or to let a bull toss me, or to stand behind a kicking horse" (60).

These extreme declarations are rebuked by Helen, who challenges her to check these desires. "You think too much of the love of human beings," she says. "The sovereign hand that created your frame, and put life into it, has provided you with other resources than your feeble self, or than creatures feeble as you" (60). Helen's words become Jane's marching orders—she must learn to check her desire for approval and affection with right thinking about God, herself, and others.

---

unattractive. The intellect is also prized highly in our heroines, and virtue takes the back seat, which, ironically, eliminates true intellect.

As the story progresses, Jane excels in her studies and in her ability to rule over her spirit. Although her awareness of injustices remain, it moves from sentiments of retribution to ones of social change. After having taught at Lowood school for many years, she dreams of other options besides that of being a teacher. She tells her readers, "I tired of the routine of eight years in one afternoon. I desired liberty; for liberty I gasped; for liberty I uttered a prayer; it seemed scattered on the wind faintly blowing" (74). What kind of liberty is this? It seems a little ambiguous on the page, but remember the limits put on women at this point in history. Higher education was not an option for her, nor were any other occupations beyond teaching or being a governess. Jane feels these societal restrictions deeply. She soliloquizes:

> Women are supposed to be very calm generally; but women feel just as men feel; they need exercise for their faculties and a field for their efforts as much as their brothers do; they suffer from too rigid a stagnation, precisely as men would suffer; and it is too narrow-minded in their more privileged fellow-creatures to say that they ought to confine themselves to making puddings and knitting stockings, to playing on the piano and embroidering bags. (96)

Is this a sign of discontentment and whining? An argument could be made along those lines. Yet if Jane did not slam up against her Victorian culture, rightly criticized for its many restrictive and wrong-headed views of women—she would be a little less realistic. Contentment does not mean seeing no evil, but rather trusting that God is in control of it all. Leaving these thoughts out would make Jane significantly less human.

Knowing that there is not much she can do about it, Jane opts for a position as a governess at Thornfield Manor. It is there that Jane exchanges daydreams of societal change, too large a project to take on, for a more manageable dream. At Thornfield, Jane strives to fulfill her desire for freedom and societal change within her relationship with Edward Rochester.

Romantic love is the main vehicle through which Jane's character is tested. This might seem like a shallow move on Charlotte Brontë's part. Why does Jane's character have to be "proven" through a relationship? Why doesn't she slay a dragon or smash a glass ceiling? Brontë makes this choice because she knows that a woman's character is *most* tried through her relationships, the most dramatic of which being with whomever she marries. Romances, therefore, are not just for ditzes and dumb-dumbs.[14] How men and women conduct themselves when they come together are the stories that builds societies, whether for good or evil. Their actions set the trajectory for how society will behave afterward.

Jane and Rochester's love story is revealing on a couple levels. First, it tells us what Jane believes about the nature

---

14. Although they can be.

of romantic love. It is depicted as a power outside of one's control. Jane assures her readers that she clearly sees the bombastic, manipulative, heavy-breathing Rochester, but falls for him anyway. "I had not forgotten his faults," she says. "He was proud, sardonic, harsh to inferiority of every description" (129). She walks into the situation with her eyes open and her judgment working. In addition, Rochester is unattainable as her employer and as someone of higher social status, yet she still loves him. He pursues another woman right in front of her, which would indicate either he has no intention of returning her affection or that he is immature and a waste of time. Yet, she still loves him. "I had not intended to love him," she says. "The reader knows I had wrought hard to extirpate from my soul the germs of love there detected." But these germs of love prove too infectious. They grow and spread and eventually take over until she confesses, "while I breathe and think I must love him" (154). It appears as though, against her will and out of her control, Jane is infatuated with Rochester. Furthermore, because Brontë presents love as an uncontrollable, dominating emotion, Jane becomes a victim, even a martyr, and her romantic suffering takes on a noble quality.

This mentality of romantic love is a dangerous one. If love is a power outside of oneself, then a person in love is not entirely responsible for his or her actions. How many TV dramas are based on this premise? Delusional friendlationships, lapses in judgment, creepy emotional affairs, and even adultery itself are given passes because those caught in the grip of romantic love cannot help themselves.[15]

The second thing Jane's romance with Rochester tells us is what she actually wants. Rochester is an ideal romantic candidate for Jane because he professes to her what she believes about herself—that she is his equal. More than passion, affection, status or wealth, it seems as though equality is for Jane a necessary condition for romance to flourish.

However, once Rochester begins to step into the role of "Provider," she becomes dissatisfied with their relationship. Her idea of "equality" actually involves something more than respect (158). We see a shift in their relationship after Rochester proposes to Jane and they become committed to each other. When Rochester attempts to buy a bunch of fancy dresses for her, Jane becomes irritated. "His smile was such as a sultan might, in a blissful and fond moment, bestow on a slave his gold and gems had enriched" (236). He has become a master, and she a slave. She continues, "The more he bought me, the more

---

15. In *The Screwtape Letters*, C.S. Lewis really nails this point: "If he is an emotional, gullible man, feed him on minor poets and fifth rate novelists of the old school until you have made him believe that 'Love' is both irresistible and somehow intrinsically meritorious. This belief is not much help, I grant you, in producing causal unchastity; but it is an incomparable recipe for prolonged, 'noble', romantic, tragic adulteries, ending, if all goes well, in murders and suicides" (1942; New York: HarperOne, 2001), 102.

my cheek burned with a sense of annoyance and degradation" (236). The more he gives materially, the more she is demoted from her status as equal. In Jane's pitiable case, at least, her fears are understandable. Given Rochester's character and history, it is reasonable to suspect he will turn out to be a tyrant and an indifferent lover as he had with his past flings and old flames, and that his lavishing of gifts is an attempt to transform her into some kind of a doll rather than a companion.

Jane attempts to address this problem by contriving some separate identity from her husband. The only way she can conceive of doing this is through economic independence.[16] She offers to stay on as Adele's governess, maintaining a salary from Rochester (237). But this won't work, and they both know it. It's a real pin to their romance bubble.

In order for Brontë to ensure Jane's equality in her romance with Rochester, Brontë kills off the relationship between them and raises it up again. This is no random move. Brontë was a clergyman's daughter. She knew the solution for a happily ever after can only be found through death and resurrection. In a twist that has been accused of being a *deus ex machina*, Brontë gives us the circumstances necessary for Jane Eyre to thrive in her marriage with

---

16. Of course, taken to an extreme, this is not a biblical sentiment. After all, the husband is charged with the responsibility of being the financial breadwinner (1 Tim. 5:8), and whether or not a wife makes money should not drive a wedge between her and her husband.

Edward Rochester. When Jane and Rochester are brought back together, Bertha is dead, Rochester's grand palace and his wealth are diminished, and he is blind and crippled. As for Jane, after having lost everything she formerly knew, and literally almost dying on the Rivers' doorsteps, she gains family, friends, and a large, unexpected inheritance. She becomes economically independent, and Rochester becomes physically dependent on her.

While Charlotte Brontë had something right about her method for achieving change (death and resurrection of the things her characters prided themselves on the most), the relationship she brings back from the dead is a strange, sickly romantic union. She resurrects a Frankenstein, where the man in the marriage is crippled, helpless, and metaphysically impotent. And who is Jane at the end of it all? Reader, she is "indomitable."

Jane's indomitability is one of the main themes of the book and the ideal into which Jane Eyre is growing. The theme of indomitability is displayed most clearly at the climax of the novel, when Jane discovers the existence of Rochester's insane wife and wrestles with herself to do the right thing. "Who in the world cares for you? [she asks herself] Or who will be injured by what you do? Still indomitable was the reply—I care for myself. The more solitary, the more friendless, the more unsustained I am, the more I will respect myself. I will keep the law given by God; sanctioned by man."

This idea is repeated at the end of the novel, this time by Rochester, who confirms this growth in her,[17] that she is "indomitable." At this point, we can see that her desire for freedom and equality have morphed into a desire for autonomy. Her passions, her person, her convictions are her own and cannot be affected by an "other." She wants to give herself in marriage and keep an identity apart from her husband. With a large fortune and a handicapped lover, Jane can marry Rochester without becoming dependent on him, thus preserving her autonomy.

This is where we can detect a dose of secular humanism in Brontë's worldview. The plot teaches us that Jane's autonomy is of the greatest importance. Brontë has found a way for Jane to give herself without losing herself, which is no gift at all. Having come to this conclusion, both critics and fans are quick to say, "so, yeah, Charlotte Brontë and Jane Eyre are feminists." But a cursory glance at some of Jane's actions and thoughts shows us she defies some of modern feminism's main tenets. For example, she does not dismiss the domestic arts. She tells St. John Rivers they are "some of the best pleasures on earth." This means her desire to do more in her society does not degrade domesticity. Furthermore, Jane is obviously no advocate of free-love, as were some of Charlotte's contemporaries and

---

17. Karen Swallow Prior, "Jane Eyre and the Invention of the Self," *The Atlantic*, March 3, 2016, accessed December 14, 2016, http://www.theatlantic.com/entertainment/archive/2016/03/how-jane-eyre-created-the-modern-self/460461/.

female writers before her. Jane's refusal to be with Rochester in an unlawful way because of her sense of self-respect
and the "law given by God; sanctioned by man" shows
this. Lastly, her reliance on Providence is her source for
overcoming trials. So whatever shortcomings and strange
ideas exist in the novel, a charitable reader can conclude
that some of Charlotte Brontë's concerns for the injustices
in her society and toward women were biblical. In fact, it
could be said that her imagination was perhaps just too
confined and repressed to envision a better solution.

Part of the appeal of *Jane Eyre* is that Jane's desires and
fears are still shared by women today. Many women have
sought, as she did, to contrive some sense of self-esteem
and separate identity within themselves while at the same
time attempting to satisfy a desire for home and husband
within a biblical framework. The ultimate answer to this
is that, if a woman is in Christ, she is free. That means
a woman's identity is not determined by where she is in
history, what injustices she suffers, what very real evils she
has to face in her particular circumstances. Neither is a
woman's identity dependent on her husband, be he good
or bad. A woman's worth and identity is rooted in God.
Because of this, we can give ourselves away, without fear
for ourselves, knowing that God has secured our identity
in His "indomitable" Son.

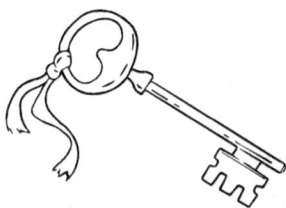

QUOTABLES

1. "Do you think, because I am poor, obscure, plain and little, I am soulless and heartless? You think wrong!—I have as much soul as you,—and full as much heart! And if God had gifted me with some beauty and much wealth, I should have made it as hard for you to leave me, as it is now for me to leave you!"

    ~ Jane Eyre, Ch. 23, p. 222

2. "I care for myself. The more solitary, the more friendless, the more unsustained I am, the more I will respect myself."

    ~ Jane Eyre, Ch. 27, p. 279

3. "It is in vain to say human beings ought to be satisfied with tranquility: they must have action; and they will make it if they cannot find it. Millions are condemned to a stiller doom than mine, and millions are in silent revolt against their lot. Nobody knows how many

rebellions besides political rebellions ferment in the masses of life which people earth. Women are supposed to be very calm generally: but women feel just as men feel; they need exercise for their faculties, and a field for their efforts, as much as their brothers do; they suffer from too rigid a restraint, to absolute a stagnation, precisely as men would suffer; and it is narrow-minded in their more privileged fellow-creatures to say that they ought to confine themselves to making puddings and knitting stockings, to playing on the piano and embroidering bags. It is thoughtless to condemn them, or laugh at them, if they seek to do more or learn more than custom has pronounced necessary for their sex."

~ Jane Eyre, Ch. 12, p. 96

4.   "Reader, I married him."

~ Jane Eyre, Ch. 38, p. 395

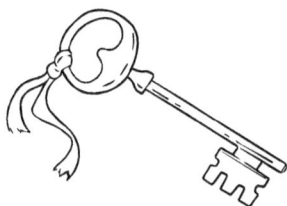

21 SIGNIFICANT QUESTIONS AND ANSWERS

1. *Jane Eyre* is narrated from a first person point of view. Does this make us more or less trusting towards Jane?

    It makes us more trusting of Jane. The first-person style reads like a journal entry, intimate and confessional. The fact that the narrator frequently stops to address her "reader" creates the sense that we are engaged in a conversation with someone who is confiding some very weighty and personal matters. In this situation, it can be very easy to let the narrator tell you what to think about herself and the characters around her without evaluating whether or not her actions and the actions of others line up with what is true and biblical.

2.   What are the Gothic elements of this book?

> There are many. First, Jane suffers horrific abuse from
> the Reed family and Mr. Brocklehurst. Then there
> are the gloomy descriptions of the moors and of
> Thornfield mansion, and the mentioning of ghosts in
> the red room and in Thornfield. There's also the eerie,
> twilight journeys Jane takes to and from Thornfield,
> as well as her walks around the mansion's misty
> grounds. Mr. Rochester is a brooding, tormented
> spirit. The ominous presence in Thornfield, thought
> to be a ghost, turns out to be Rochester's monstrous
> and insane wife, Bertha. All of these elements com-
> bined with the romance between Jane and Rochester
> contribute to its Gothic character.[18]

3.   What is Edward Rochester like? Is he Jane's ideal
     romantic prospect?

> Jane describes Rochester as "changeful and abrupt"
> (112). He is emotionally manipulative, playing
> creepy mind-games to get Jane to reveal her true
> feelings for him. For instance, he commanded her
> to sit and watch as he acted out a marriage cha-
> rade with Blanche Ingram. Not long after this,
> Rochester disguises himself as a fortune teller in an
> attempt to get Jane to confess her feelings for him.
> Not exactly an honest-dealing or straight-forward
> man.
>
> Rochester is oftentimes described as passionate
> and on the verge of violence. For example, when

---

18. Krueger, 39.

Jane discovers Bertha and is considering whether or not to leave Rochester, he grabs her, keeping a painful hold on her arm and waist, and deliberates whether or not to forcefully take her (279-280). This kind of behavior is not romantic, no matter how strongly either party feels. This behavior is destructive and evil.

Even though Rochester is humbled by his wife's suicide and his own physical crippling, his character is not one worth Jane waiting around to see if he'll change. The book of Proverbs 22:24 says to "make no friendship with an angry man, and with a furious man thou shalt not go." This is a good rule of thumb to remember when considering someone for marriage: if that person is angry, don't date them. And another rule, for the other thumb, is to be able to identify an angry character before forming a strong emotional attachment which compromises your judgment.

4. How is physical beauty regarded in this book? Is this an accurate way to think about physical beauty?

Throughout most of the novel, physical beauty is used as a literary device to highlight a character's inner ugliness. If a character possesses physical beauty, he or she most likely lacks depth, is probably of a higher social status, and is most likely some kind of hypocrite. Take, for instance, the ladies of Mr. Brocklehurst's family. Their heads are covered in ringlets, the same type that Mr. Brocklehurst rages against to his low-income tenants.

The same goes for the belle, Lady Ingram, whom Mr. Rochester brings in to make Jane jealous. Consider this passage:

"She was very showy, but she was not genuine: she had a fine person, many brilliant attainments; but her mind was poor, her heart barren by nature; nothing bloomed spontaneously on that soil; no unforced natural fruit delighted by its freshness. She was not good; she was not original: she used to repeat sounding phrases from books: she never offered, nor had, an opinion of her own. She advocated a high tone of sentiment; but she did not know the sensations of sympathy and pity; tenderness and truth were not in her" (163).

While beauty *can* be associated with a lack of depth (the stereotype doesn't come from nowhere), we should tread very carefully before making a call on someone's character based on how they appear. When we read these passages revealing a character's inner struggles, it is important to keep in mind that these descriptions are supposedly coming from Jane and her first-person perspective. When she tells us that Lady Ingram is "a mark beneath jealousy: she was too inferior to incite the feeling," (163) we shouldn't rush to believe her. The pitfalls for a plain person are the same as they are for a beautiful one—pride, with the added element of self-deceived envy. The Bible does not use physical appearance to reveal the heart and it has no problem pointing out physical beauty as traits of its heroes and heroines. Think of David, Abigail, Sarah, etc.

5. Where does classism appear in Jane Eyre? What does Jane believe is an answer to prejudice?

> Classism appears all throughout the novel. It is apparent at Lowood, where the low-income students are expected to physically display their class by dressing plainly and humbly, in comparison to the Brocklehurst ladies of higher social standing, who are given a pass to dress ornately. Mrs. Fairfax remarks about John and Mary (servants at Thornfield) "they are only servants, and one can't converse with them on terms of equality: one must keep them at due distance, for fear of losing one's authority" (84). We also see this in the Ingrams et al treating Jane as an outlier and part of an inferior class.
>
> Jane believes that education is a cure for the classism and stubborn prejudices she sees in her society. "Prejudices, it is well known, are most difficult to eradicate from the heart whose soil has never been loosened or fertilised by education: they grow there, firm as weeds among stones" (229). Ironically, Jane's constant reference to the superiority or inferiority of the minds around her is a mere bait-and-switch of one set of prejudices for another. There's really no cure for any societal ill apart from the Gospel. No matter how good something is, apart from Christ, people will always find a way to pervert it.

6.   What kind of role does Providence play throughout the book? Is it a significant or minor role? Do the references to Providence "work" with the plot?

> Providence is an unseen character in the novel who is oftentimes indirectly responsible for moving the story forward. The story's plot hinges on moments where Providence aides Jane in making decisions (i.e., looking for a governess position, helping her leave Rochester after she finds out about his wife, and returning to Rochester after a season). Many of these moments are subtle and it can be easy to dismiss the role of Providence as a mere nod to the conventional religion of Brontë's time. However, the discovery of Jane's relations and subsequent wealth, the burning down of Thornfield, the death of Bertha, and the humbling of Rochester—in other words, all the major plot points—are actions attributed to Providence.
>
> Providence's role in moving the plot along only works if you actually believe in a God that interacts with people and is the One setting up their stories.

7.   What is phrenology and how does it affect Jane's perspective of the people around her?

> Phrenology was the faddish 19th-century pseudoscience that claimed to be able to measure people's character and intellect based on the way their heads were shaped. This quack "science" is all throughout *Jane Eyre*. Jane oftentimes relies on it to describe the people around her, and to confirm her insights about them. For example, she tells us that

she herself has a "considerable organ of Veneration," (40) she describes Blanche Ingram as having a "low brow," which would indicate a lack of intellect (think opposite of high-brow). Rochester is described as having "a solid enough mass of intellectual organs, but an abrupt deficiency where the suave sign of benevolence should have arisen" (116).

Jane falls back on this science to confirm her insights about people and, as in the case of Blanche Ingram, it's all too easy to dismiss people absolutely and vilify them. It can be tempting to want to rely on something so seemingly certain as science to discern people's characters and intellects, but this is a dangerous game. Once you start dismissing people as "less-than" on a purely physical "scientific" basis, you get terrible dehumanization.

8. What does fire symbolize in the book?

What does it *not* symbolize? Brontë uses fire in an almost willy-nilly fashion to portray passion, romance and its dangers if unchecked, as well as sanity, repression, and the like.

9. Why is the character Adele important to the story?

The presence of Adele assures the readers that Rochester is not entirely a pig. Taking responsibility for the illegitimate daughter of his former cheating lover exhibits a sense of benevolence and love.

10. In what ways is passion regarded in the book?

> From the religious perspective, passion is a vice that
> needs to be expelled. Think of Mrs. Reed punishing
> Jane for her impassioned reaction to John Reed's
> bullying, or consider St. John River's commitment
> to a stoic view of life and love. To Jane, howev-
> er, passion is a natural part of her being, and one
> that needs to be moderated by right thinking and
> vice versa. Jane comments on this when she says,
> "Feeling without judgment is a washy draught
> indeed; but judgment untempered by feeling is too
> bitter and husky a morsel for human deglutition"
> (208).

11. What evidence does Rochester give for Bertha being
    crazy? Was she really crazy?

> Rochester describes Bertha in the early years of
> their marriage as having a "common, low, narrow
> mind," "obnoxious taste," given to "outbreaks of .
> . . violent and unreasonable temper." And finally,
> as "her character ripened," Rochester accuses her
> of being "intemperate" and "unchaste," just like
> her Mama. Throwing fits of temper, committing
> adultery, and lacking self-control hardly pass as
> symptoms of a mental disease nowadays, but in
> Victorian England, these traits were considered a
> form of moral madness.[19] A key to understanding
> this mentality is to know what they thought about

---

19. Carol Atherton, "The figure of Bertha Mason," *British Library* (2016).

sin. In a letter to W.S. William, Charlotte Brontë observes that "sin is itself a species of insanity."[20] Taking a look at Bertha when she is discovered, she really seems legitimately crazy, but how she got that way—whether it was inherited from her family or a vice she indulged that took over her mind—is debatable.

12. Are Bertha's actions throughout the book in any way rational?

There are several times when Bertha creeps around the house: she sets fire to Rochester's bed while he's asleep. Another time, on the night before Jane and Rochester's wedding, she enters Jane's bedroom and tears her wedding veil. She attacks her brother, the one who supposedly set her up with Rochester, when he came to visit. These actions do not seem senseless. They actually make a little bit of sense for a bitter woman who has been locked up by her husband.

13. How are religious men portrayed in *Jane Eyre*?

Religious men are typically seen as hypocrites and manipulators. They are concerned with maintaining empty traditions that contradict the Bible. Mr. Brocklehurst is the first example. We see his double-standards when he rages against a student's curly hair—

20. Brontë, *Selected Letters of Charlotte Brontë*, ed. Margaret Smith (Oxford: OUP, 2007), 96 [January 4, 1948].

"Why has she or any other, curled hair? Why,
in defiance of every precept and principle of this
house, does she conform to the world so openly—
here in an evangelical, charitable establishment—as
to wear her hair one mass of curls?"

"Julia's hair curls naturally," returned Miss
Temple.

"Naturally! Yes, but we are not to conform to nature: I wish these girls to be the children of Grace."
And then of course, there's St. John Rivers, who
wants to marry Jane for her work abilities.

14. Is St. John Rivers a godly man?

Despite his name, the answer to this question is
debatable. Whether or not readers are supposed to
admire or despise him is harder to determine. On
the one hand, Jane talks about him in very down-
to-earth terms, acknowledging that he is merely
human alongside herself. She shows his ugly side,
and comments on his character knowingly the way
she does with Edward Rochester. And yet, there is
still the sense that St. John Rivers is a hero of sorts.
She admits to Mary that he is a "good man" and later a "great one." She acknowledges and affirms the
extreme asceticism exhibited by St. John by denying
himself to become a missionary and dying early as
a high and sacred calling, one that is condoned by
Providence. But this is not how God operates. He
does not call us to extreme pietism which disregards
practical considerations such as (not to be insensi-
tive here) whether or not you have the constitution
to be a missionary in India without dying.

15. Does Jane's longing for a change in society's view of women exclude domesticity?

> No. In fact, in the passage where St. John Rivers tries to convince Jane to marry him, challenging her to "look higher than domestic endearments and household joys." To which she responds, "The best things the world has!"[21] It is interesting to note that it is the extremely pious and ascetic Rivers, not the worldly Rochester, who dismisses domesticity. Jane wants to find a balance.

16. Can you see evidence of *Jane Eyre* affecting culture downstream from itself?

> The novel has certainly influenced how society thinks about women and how we portray them in literature. *Jane Eyre* prizes intelligence and education in women and affirms these qualities as leading to more robust virtues, which was a challenge to Brontë's culture. Today, this emphasis on intelligence and education has been distorted. In our culture, "intellect" is the main thing that distinguishes an "empowered" woman, and other virtues have been divorced from it. For us to admire a female character, it really doesn't matter if she is wise, self-controlled, or loyal, so long as she is intelligent. This usually means she'll have lots of degrees, at least one per brain cell. Furthermore, we can point

---

21. Charlotte Brontë and Stevie Davies, *Jane Eyre* (London: Penguin Classics, 2008), 451.

to Jane's acclaimed "search for self"[22] journey as
being influential in today's trend of authenticity and
the "find yourself" movement.

17. Many have called Edward Rochester a Byronic Hero. Is
Jane a Byronic Hero too?

Jane has some striking Byronic qualities. She is
frequently misunderstood. She's in some ways tor-
mented by her society and her own desires. She's an
artist (painter) and her art is dark and romantic. At
a certain point in the novel, she carries a mysterious
past that she does not want to be revealed.

18. Should you like this story? What is there to appreciate
about it?

For one thing, the story's prose is beautiful. The
fact that Brontë can maintain such an elevated,
poetic voice and still communicate with crystal
clarity is an impressive feat. The story also captures
certain parts of human nature very well. Brontë
obviously understands certain elements of human
nature (especially that of women). She also knows
religious pride and captures its trappings well in
St. John River's character. One wonders whether
she's ever encountered a normal, spiritually healthy

---

22. Karen Swallow Prior, "Jane Eyre and the Invention of the
Self," *The Atlantic*, March 3, 2016, accessed December 14, 2016,
http://www.theatlantic.com/entertainment/archive/2016/03/
how-jane-eyre-created-the-modern-self/460461/.

man in her life—but she does understand the
oddballs.

19. Some have made comparisons between *Jane Eyre* and
rubbish like *Twilight* and *50 Shades of Grey* because
they seem to revolve around the romance between an
unattainable, vicious male and an unsuspecting, but
totally willing, mousy female. Is this a true comparison?

> At first glance, these novels seem to share simi-
> lar characters and themes. Unattainability is the
> common hitch that creates conflict and makes the
> romance interesting. For many people this sim-
> ilarity is enough to dismiss *Jane Eyre* as kitschy
> trash. But it's important to know the reason for the
> unattainability. Does God prohibit this romance in
> the Bible? Is the lead male unattainable because he
> is a sparkly demon-vampire wanting to transform
> the girl into a demon-vampire to live sparkly ever
> after? Is he unattainable because he is a sadist with
> a satanic sexual appetite? Christians may not join
> hands with the wicked and be unequally yoked with
> an unbeliever. Demonic vampires and sadists are
> out, and Christians are right to object.
>
> But the situation in *Jane Eyre* is different. For
> the first half of the book, the reason why Rochester
> is unattainable to Jane, or so she thinks, is because
> Rochester is her employer and he is of higher social
> status than she. Admittedly, the employer/employee
> scenario can get icky, but it's not necessarily a bib-
> lically disqualifying situation. Jane's society forbids
> a man of high social status and income to marry a

girl from the poor side of the tracks. But this is not
a moral reason for two people to avoid marriage.
We, along with Jane, should not want to insist on
this classist rule.

When it is revealed that Rochester has been
married the whole time (i.e., he is lawfully and
biblically unattainable), Jane does what no heroine
in *Twilight* or *50 Shades* would ever do. She flees.
Literally. She recognizes that the passions she feels
for Rochester would have her do something insane
and wrong. This is a godly response (2 Tim. 2:22),
and one we should imitate and commend. Way to
go, Jane.

20. Is the book melodramatic? How?

In some ways, the Gothic elements in this book
contribute to its melodramatic spirit. The severe
treatment of Jane as a child, the madness and
death of Bertha, the maiming of Rochester (to
name but a few), add up to make the book feel
over-the-top.

But the main thing that makes *Jane Eyre* seem
melodramatic is its seriousness. With a few excep-
tions, there is a near absence of humor in the book.
Jane's emotion all happen to be on the incredibly
heavy side and Jane takes herself and her romance
very, very seriously.

When romance becomes entirely serious,
(which is to say when people take themselves too
seriously) there is no room for laughing at yourself
and, God forbid, others laughing at you. In this

very serious world, characters don't have that very human mix of foibles and ridiculousness that make average men and women endearing. Instead, the characters must be heavy and dark and straight-faced. This, fortunately, isn't like real life.

21. How is *Jane Eyre* like a fairy tale? How is it not?

The story follows a classic fairytale structure, like Cinderella, where a poor orphan rises in society through marriage and riches. *Jane Eyre* itself alludes to the fairy tale Bluebeard, the story of a wealthy man whose current wife discovers the remains of all his past wives locked up in back room of his house. Although this story ends in a marriage, Brontë gives her fairy tale a twist. Jane receives her wealth and consequent new social status through an inheritance, not marriage, and she is the one who goes after Rochester and in some ways saves him from his distress.

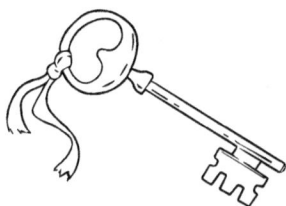

FURTHER DISCUSSION
AND REVIEW

Master what you have read by reviewing and integrating the different elements of this classic.

SETTING AND CHARACTERS
Be able to compare and contrast the personalities (including strengths, weaknesses, and mannerisms) of each character. How does the setting affect the characters?

PLOT
Be able to describe the beginning, middle, and end of the book along with specific details that move the plot forward and make it compelling. This includes the success or downfall (or both) of each character.

CONFLICT
Go through the character list and describe the tension between any and all main characters. Then, think about

whether any characters have internal conflict (in their own minds). Is there any overt conflict (fighting), or conflict with impersonal forces?

THEME STATEMENTS

Be able to describe what this classic is telling us about the world. Is the message true? What truth can we take from the plot, characters, conflict, and themes (even if the author didn't believe that truth)? Do any objects take on added meaning because of repetition or their place in the story (i.e., do any objects become symbols)? How does the author use perspective, tone, and irony to tell the truth?

Be able to interact with and give examples for the following theme statements:

> Unrestrained passion and romance results in heartache and self-destruction. Alternatively, the suppression of all passion leads to stoicism, asceticism, and hypocrisy.

> "Finding one's self" is never only about oneself. Unless done in the biblical way, which is to lose yourself to Christ, seeking after your own identity will always require the reshaping, and sometimes the domination, of others.

> Convention and tradition are not the same thing as truth. Just because something has been done for ages does not make it right. Convention and tradition do not have ultimate authority, so we can look to the Bible to test them both.

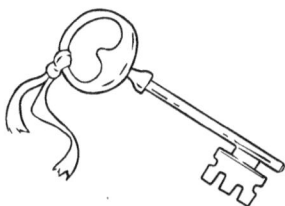

A NOTE FROM THE PUBLISHER:
TAKING THE CLASSICS QUIZ

Once you have finished the worldview guide, you can prepare for the end-of-book test. Each test will consist of a short-answer section on the book itself and the author, a short-answer section on plot and the narrative, and a long-answer essay section on worldview, conflict, and themes.

Each quiz, along with other helps, can be downloaded for free at www.canonpress.com/ClassicsQuizzes. If you have any questions about the quiz or its answers or the Worldview Guides in general, you can contact Canon Press at service@canonpress.com or 208.892.8074.

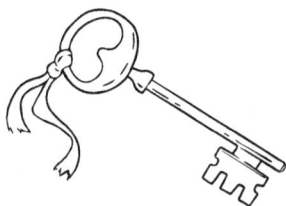

ABOUT THE AUTHOR

Amanda Ryan is a stay-at-home mom who teaches literature for Logos Online School and has written for Economic Modeling Specialists International. She has B.A.s in English and Music from the University of California and an M.A. in Theology and Letters from New Saint Andrews College. She and her husband Danny have two children.